For Dear Life

Pitt Poetry Series

Ed Ochester, Editor

For Dear Life

Ronald Wallace

University of Pittsburgh Press

Published by the University of Pittsburgh Press, Pittsburgh, Pa., 15260
Copyright © 2015, Ronald Wallace
All rights reserved
Manufactured in the United States of America
Printed on acid-free paper
10 9 8 7 6 5 4 3 2 1
ISBN 13: 978-0-8229-6386-8
ISBN 10: 0-8229-6386-8

for Margaret

Contents

III. For Dear Life

I.

In the Great Scheme of Things

Thank God

Adam and Eve were bored; they were boring.
Eden was no Eden, after all. Where were
the restaurants, the music halls, the movies?
Where were the children to badger and tax them?
The illnesses to keep them in check?
The weather for something to talk about?
The sins of the body to share? Funny, but
there was only so much pleasure
one could get from perfection, so much
sustenance from raw milk and honey.
Thank God, Eve thought, for the snake and the tree
that promised such interesting suffering!
Thank God, Adam thought, for Eve
who knew that things couldn't go on like this,
who could teach him to love pain and loss!
Thank God, God thought, He had left them
to their own best devices, so they could
get out while the getting was good!

The Fear of God

after Red Grooms, "French Bread"

The man on stilts (or are those baguettes up his pants?)
with the big French bread under his arm, seems to be
much too big for the cobblestone street,
much too big for the bright boarding house,
or is it a matter of perspective? Perhaps he's
up close? In fact, on further inspection, we see
his feet are outside of the frame! He's
superimposed on the scene—somewhere in
France, we suppose. And in our large world he
is tiny! Alarmed in an upstairs window, a woman
flings open her shutters and screams! So she's
seen us now, outside the frame where her Frenchman,
with his beam of bread, steamy and fresh from the oven,
is off on an urgent errand, determined
to deliver his implausible message. She screams,
though it seems no one else has seen us as yet
in our furtiveness, looking on: not
the bicyclist stuck to the street sweeper's head,
not the Rubinesque nude in her bower,
not the woman whose own bread is leaving the
frame as she speeds down the vanishing street.
Where has it gone? will she fretfully wonder,
as the street sweeper sweeps and sweeps,
and the little dog leans toward the
carefree young girl who's about to be lost
to a leg of our aberrant bread man
whose blue suit is moving to leave us exposed—
despite ourselves, glued to the picture—
our faces like loaves of enormous *pain ronde*
in the eyes of whomever flings wide their arms
and screams. Or prays. Or sings.

Body World

Is it art or science or spectacle?
Novelty, exhibit, or display?
This "show," shall we call it,
of body parts, the remains
of what was once demonstrably
human, all the fluids, the juices,
removed, the small breath—the
soul, shall we call it?—snuffed.
Has immortality come to this?
The archer, the hurdler, the
cardplayer, the bride, the
spear-thrower, the equestrian—
plasticized®? Oh yes, there's
the history of anatomy, postered
on all of the walls, the public
displays of dissection centuries
past, the rapt crowds preening
for a closer look, an afternoon's
grim entertainment. There's
Leonardo carting the dead bodies
home, wrist deep in fleshy debris,
death's detritus, dripping with
vessel and nerve, intent on his
exquisite sketches. And Fragonard,
the darling of Paris, with his skinned
and shellacked seventeenth-century
dead horse. And yet, they *are*
beautiful, in their own way, these
sculptures of muscle and ligament,
capillary, neuron, and bone,
stripped of all posturing and
pretence, these silent reminders
that heaven and hell are not so
far apart, that when art has its way
with science, their progeny might not

be unlike this—think *miracle,* think
divine intervention, think *Red Sea,*
think *pillar of salt.* Think Death with
His intelligent designs on us, with
only our best interests at heart.

The Knowing

What you don't know won't hurt you
was what they said when what they meant
was that they weren't going to tell you
something you wanted to know, meant

it was none of your business, meant
you were out of the loop, dismissed, you
were extraneous, a third wheel, a nonentity, meant
nothing in the great scheme of things. You

were irrelevant, or so you thought.
Now that you know, you wish you didn't—
all those things that hurt you. You thought
you were immune to the cancer that didn't

remiss, the stroke, the pneumonia that didn't
mind its own business, the old age you thought
belonged only to the already old. Why didn't
you just let go what you needed to know (you thought)?

Bed Wetter

They let me believe that
I had wet the bed.
We were in a motel.
I was four, or five, we
were on our way
to Minnesota, perhaps,
the lake, our first
vacation. I was excited.
We were sharing the
bed. Times were hard.
It was 1950. They
kept a monthly budget
by slipping bills into
a business envelope
when they cashed their
checks at the local savings
bank. When I woke up
after midnight, the bed
was wet. I was
too old for that, I knew.
I lay still not wanting to
wake them, not wanting them
to know. So when they said
my name like it was
an embarrassment,
well, *yes,* it must have been
me! Who else *could* it
have been? They were
grown-ups after all. They
were so nice about it. They
said they understood, they
kissed me with
a smile, stripped the clammy
sheets, found something—
a spare blanket, perhaps,

for the rest of the sleepless
night. *I had wet the bed.*
I'd carry that embarrassment
with me like a false friend,
who'd tag along behind me
all my doggy life.
This was before
his MS was apparent, before
the cane and crutches, before
the wheelchair, the muscle loss,
the falls and "accidents"
I found myself mopping up
after. Maybe they didn't know.
Maybe it really was me.
And so I took the blame, took
the mortification, the lie, *if* a
lie, a small lie, I now know, as
the lies of the great world go.
Though sixty-five long years later
I find myself
back in that bed with them, my
parents, all the love I knew,
secure in the bed between them,
my whole life spreading
before me, the warmth
in the bed spreading toward me,
with its lessons of loss and
betrayal deposited in the bank,
so pungent and sour and rank.

Catching My Father

Hey, you want to play catch?
he'd say. And though that was the last
thing I wanted to do, *Sure,* I'd reply,
and follow him and his wheelchair
out of the small apartment
into the courtyard, where,
self-conscious and embarrassed, I'd
throw him the wayward ball
as he strained to keep up the appearance
that he could somehow snag and return it.
I was eight, but both of us knew
we were just doing what we had to:
he was my father; I was his son.
And that's what fathers and sons do.
But whenever the neighbor,
on his two good legs, would show up
to take over the fatherly duties,
throwing our world off-balance,
my father would wilt, and roll
slowly away on his two wheels
into the waiting dark, waving
me into the future, and I'd go.
How could I know I'd be sitting here, now,
in my own motionless chair, alone
in the extra innings, wanting only
to catch him with my best stuff,
as he brushes off all of my signs.

The Day My Father Said "Shit"

I was twelve, in the back
of the car with my grandmother.
They'd told her it was just
a drive in the country. A beautiful
day, though she sat hunched by the door
like a bird clutched tight to its branch,
her own fractured song chirping
up in her throat. We knew something
was up, she and I, but what?
The sun shone as it must. The August
breeze was hot. My mother was silent.
My father's small hum. And then
we were there, on the lawn of
The Home, the terror in my grandmother's
eyes like an alarm that would never go off.
The door opened and shut
like a shot at a dove in hunting season,
and "Shit!" my father said. "Shit!"
And we left her alone, to her own
devices, her whole world exploded,
and drove off into the future she'd left
that was not just
a drive in the country. And they left
me there, too, or part of me—how could they
have known?—before I could
properly sing, alone
on the page where my grandmother wrote
what little she could,
clutched to the branch of my throat.

Wolf Pack

after Socho

One night when I was twelve and alone in the
house, I rifled through my father's room. The moon
bloomed in his open window. I knew that this
was wrong, but I was simply bored, the evening
slow and long, and, well, I was newly twelve and
looking for nothing in particular, nothing on
my mind, when suddenly I came upon the
first "wolf pack" I'd ever seen: the whole
deck full of naked 1940s women. My eyes wide,
I riffled through the nudes. Outside the sky
brightened as the moon shone in. So not
what I would have expected of my father. In a
wheelchair all his life, he never showed a trace
of guilty pleasure. Who was this man I'd stripped of
love? Outside, the moon removed its blouse of cloud.

Scrabble

Father, how I wanted you to win,
your clumsy thumbs knocking over the holder,
or jostling the board past recognition,
squinting at the blurred, recalcitrant letters
with your one good eye. I'd wait
for hours while you dozed or pondered
your next play, then help you with a word
or, adding double to your score, I'd cheat.

But I was always the one with all
the seven letter words—*miracle, healthy*—
as yours got shorter and shorter—
and, for, but, or—
until the board was blocked beyond entry
and you no longer cared about the score.

God's Grace

Multiple Sclerosis: a chronic degenerative disease of the central
nervous system . . . thought to be caused by a defect in the immune
system that may be of genetic or viral origin.

Or, as my father thought, it could be a punishment
from God, in his case for being a bastard. Literally
a bastard, born out of wedlock to a farmhand whose
sin caused a farm wife to hang herself
out behind the barn, an act that sent
reverberations down the decades, specifically
through the myelin on his spine so he would lose
his legs but not his faith. His failing health

no cause for doubt, or rage, or blasphemy;
instead, he saw it as an occasion for praise.
Praise God for logic and consistency.
Praise God for following through on his sure promise
to punish the heathen and send his only son
to redeem the sinner with nails slammed through his spine.

In the Name of God

O Great One, O Unsayable
Name, Creator of All Things
Visible and Invisible,
O Most High and Merciful
Absence, hear my prayer.
How must I address You?
You of the Improbable Moniker,
Utmost, Unlikely Entity,
Enormous Essence, Lord
I do not know. O
Gap, O Blank, O Nothingness
Most Holy. Lowdown
Intangible Non-Presence, O
for a handle by which to grab You,
some designation, some
patronymic to parse You,
to nail You, to pin You down.

Pantoum of the Prodigal Son

I think he must have understood
the story of the prodigal son.
I must confess I never could.
So when the maudlin pastor spun

his story of the prodigal son,
I rolled my eyes at my father's sighing.
Yes, when the tiresome pastor spun
his tales, my father sick and dying,

I rolled my eyes at my father's sighing.
I'd always stayed at one remove
from his sickness and his dying.
I couldn't show my love—

I'd always stayed at one remove—
and though it seems so very sad,
I couldn't show my love
because he was my dad.

Yes, though it seems so very sad,
I must confess I never could.
Because he was my dad
I think he must have understood.

Time after Time

And why should time move forward?
Do we prefer it that way?
Leaving all the grief and sorrow of the past—
the wars, the illnesses, the losses—
to accumulate like so much dust
swept under the rug, so much detritus
pushed off into some dark closet, some
out of the way corner or attic
we'll never revisit?

           Ah, the future,
always up there ahead of us
in the sunlight, too bright quite
to see, but beckoning, beckoning,
as if we were on a journey from
darkness into light, from dustiness
and decay, all those moldering remains,
to the luster of newness and wonder.

And why, like the mirage in the desert,
does the future always seem to be moving
off, always the same distance up there
ahead of us, the present, or what is
left of it, stymied at every stop, always
forgetting the path to the future, finding
its way unerringly into the past?

The Biography of Nostalgia

They met in a school
that has since gone to condos,
kissed on a doorstep
that has been condemned,

had sex in a car
now long on the rust heap,
towed off for penance
or parts. They had no

offspring, unless you call
offspring the long moony days
he spent looking after her
memory, the nights his life

lay sleepless beside him,
teaching long ago and far away
to speak. And what kind
of a life was this, in which

every book had been read
every good movie seen,
every day spent entertaining
regret, the grandchild of dream.

And was he our father
who took longing to wife,
made melancholy his business,
trafficked in properties of loss?

Elsewise and elsewhere
were where he was happiest,
the heart of the present
the past, where he carried on

while we carried on here
in a world that was going fast.

Modes of Transport

And how do I find myself
driving down Delmar, west,
the reverse of the way I,
nearly fifty years ago, walked
home from a long slow day
of eighth grade and her in my
arms again, laughing as we
careened through our heedless
childhood, all heat and flesh and
foreplay. *Put me down!* she said,
as we slid toward our lives,
Put me down! and, God help me,
I did.

Driving now against traffic
I think I might be
walking home still
in some alternate universe
where time goes its own
slow way, regardless of us
and our foolish demands
to leave all this sweetness
behind. And yes! There I am!
Walking, jaunty, along
with her, bobbing and weaving,
barely aware of the old guy
driving by so fast
with his carload of longing
he hardly has time to wave.

Geologic

Greater love has no one than this . . .

A man fell in love with a rock.
For awhile, he admired it from afar.
He swooned over it all day.
He mooned over it all night.
When he finally got up the courage
to reveal himself to the rock, the rock
played coy. The rock looked in
the other direction. The rock
was adamant, unmovable.
The rock remained stone-faced.
The rock had a heart of stone.
But the man would not be put off.
The man would not let himself be
stuck between the rock and a hard place.
He wooed the rock.
He took the rock places the rock
would never have gone without him.
He showed the rock the world.
Over time, the rock's
resistance began to erode. The man
took the rock home; the man
set up house with the rock. The rock
never complained, the rock
never talked back. The man
ate with the rock; he slept with
the rock. He prayed with the
silent rock. And so life went on
in pleasant enough fashion, man
and rock, rock and man, man and rock.
The man knew that the rock would
outlive him, knew, when he died,

someone else would take up with
the rock. But, for now,
the man put his faith in the rock
to know what to do with
a grave situation, to know what to do
when he laid down his life for the rock.

The Rapture

after Basho

Did the pilot really say "I'll see you in
a future life"? We're flying over the
South China Sea, I think. Outside, the bitter
cold would kill us, or at least give us a "radish"
as my four-year-old granddaughter called the rash that
covered her bottom with what was probably bug bites
from a night spent at Bible camp. We're flying into
a thunderstorm. The lightning looks to me
like the apocalypse; the rapture, perhaps. I
am thinking how we mistake things. How the feel
of foreignness is unnerving, or at least funny. The
"future life"? A "radish"? Sometimes icy cold
can be perceived as hot. Sometimes autumn
seems like spring; the voice of God, the wind.

Good Lord

after Issa

I used to believe in God. I went to church. Oh,
it was a long time ago. Now I'm a former
altar boy, choir soloist, youth leader, renter
of ideas not my own. I believed that I
could pray all trouble away. But now I know
that Jesus is no port in any storm. It
all comes down to faith in the unseen. It all
comes down to trust in God. It all comes down
to little in the end. It all comes down to
nothing. But when, after my father's death, I visit the
church I grew up in, and sit here in the very
same pew I remember so well, before the cold
winds of logic overtook me, what do you
know? Good Lord! I almost feel what I once felt.

Shine God's Light!

after Basho

"Lightman" stands in the chancel of my mother's church. As
he walks back and forth, festooned with Christmas tree lights to
approximate . . . what? God's love?, in the front pew a
small child leaps up and, *Sit on your bottoms! God*
wants well-behaved children, Lightman calls as I
and the child *put on our listening ears!* as directed, and look
as the lights flash on and all the Bible School children get into
it: *Shine God's Light!* they all call in unison on cue as the
Lightman smiles and shines. *Think of the darkening sky,*
Lightman says, *rain and wind, a terrible storm at*
sea, all the apostles terrified. But Jesus, with his
power, says, "Peace, be still! You are all God's treasure!"
and *Shine God's Light!* my mother cries, and I am plum
out of excuses: A blind man sees. Praise blossoms.

In the Great Scheme of Things

It all comes down to
maintenance. I wish it were
otherwise—truth or beauty,
for instance, would be preferable,
but truth and beauty change
as we now know, now that
we know what we know
is specious. Nothing stays
level or true, everything decays.
The universe itself, after all
that early commotion in
the first billionth of a second
when anything was possible,
seems intent now on going
its own heedless way to
entropy and emptiness, taking
the day, as we bustle about
systematically trying to make
things stay, as if the little
details could save us, as if
painting the peeling porch,
replacing the rotted sill,
servicing the rusted car,
mending a fence or two,
could hold it all together,
eternal optimists that we are.
As if we could hold ourselves
together, refusing to give
atom and molecule their sway
for what amounts to no more
than a flicker in God's blind eye,
if by God you mean the great
uncaring fathomless mechanics

of it all, which, however, somehow
allow us in our innocence to think
we can keep it clean, keep it
sound, keep it running, keep it
contained. Ah, dear life!
It's what I'm holding on for.

II.

And Yet

Song of Myself

after Issa

I think it's enough just to sit and meditate, heedless
of the needs of others close to us and of
their perpetual demands that seem to sap the
strength from us. My doorway and the morning dew
are all I need to make my day, and that
is where I'll plan to be. And if that marks
me misanthropic, if that threatens to end our
relationship, I say that is not my problem, closing
my door. Thoreau knew how to spend the day
alone with his peas and beans and ledgers, and we
can do the same. So much for the ties that bind.
"We must find our occasions in ourselves,"
said self-reliant Thoreau. And so I'm going to sing to
myself. And the birds. And you. And one or two others.

The Andromeda Galaxy

after Basho

The older I get the more I think about death. The
first inkling I had that it was all going to end was the first
day I heard that the Andromeda Galaxy would one day,
of its own accord, collide with us. It was the first day of
spring, I think. I was seven, and nothing but spring
and childhood were on my mind. My father and
I were reading a book about space exploration, and I
keep thinking he must not have known I'd keep
thinking about it for the rest of my life. I'm thinking
about it now that I've just turned seventy, about
the last thing I dreamed of being at age seven, when the
end of the world seemed so much closer than the end
of his life or mine. Now Andromeda, like the end of
autumn, collides with us. And it's not even autumn.

Sweet Potatoes

after Basho

Life is nasty, brutish, and short: Hobbes. Ah,
it's true. I've spent a long life thinking such
thoughts. I can't remember the last time I enjoyed a
a day of pleasant forgetfulness and pleasure. Life
is full of misery, loneliness and suffering and, sweet
Jesus, it's all over much too soon: Woody Allen. Potatoes
of wisdom, these. I boil them up again
and again for dinner, so starchy and filling they are.
I don't believe in heaven, but I'm bringing a
change of underwear. Ah, mortality is a source
of such endless pleasure. It seems we never get tired of
talking about how tired we are of it all, and that's the
long and short of it. Death plants its potatoes. We harvest
its punch lines, Hobbes and Allen flashing it a moon.

You Bet Your Life

after Basho

My back is bent. I walk like Groucho Marx. This
is no joke. Pain is my companion in the autumn
of my life. Where is Harpo when I need him? Why
is Chico gone on to his rest? Margaret Dumont is
ridiculously missing. This is no night at the opera, it
is no day at the races, no monkey business. *Hello, I
must be going.* Arthritis beeps his horn. I am
stuffed into the stateroom of my body. Aging
is a wisecrack I can't master. Room Service? So
send up a larger room! Who are you going to
believe? Me, or your own eyes? I refuse to join the
club that will have me for a member. Clouds
darken my day. Hey, maybe this *is*, after all, a
joke! Say the secret word and get the bird.

The King of Jazz

Some days he simply doesn't like himself:
the old man in the mirror, crooked eye,
balding head. When did he get so bony?
When did he shrink into a wizened elf?
Mr. Snarl and Wince. Mr. Fly
by Night. He'd had such dreams! He'd do a riff
on them, a sweet reprise, if only he
could, if his whole body didn't laugh

at the idea. He used to move through the day
as if it mattered: Mr. Hotshot, Mr.
Busybody. Now he thinks he'll just retire,
like Lear, leave his kingdom to his daughter,
and take his fool self out to the heath
and jazz up the universe with his wrath.

Hunger

It had been a good day. Twenty degrees
and sun, the ice bright as diamond,
and no wind. The bluegills piled beside
the black hole through which you could
look right down to another kingdom. Now
the fish were thawing on the workbench,
coming sluggishly back to life in my
strange air, and I was whacking them
across the back to still them, the
shudder of their side fins a frantic
wave goodbye, and filleting them when
suddenly I was struck with what it must
be like to be yanked from one life to
another, in what, no matter how dumb the
animal, must approximate terror, and, mid-
swing, I stopped. My fingers slick with
air sacs, fish scales, blood, intestines.
My daughter, the vegan, swam into
view, her blue eyes wide, unblinking. I
thought about our mission on this earth,
the love of fathers for their daughters,
our long history, great and small.
But I was hungry—aren't we all?—
for the slightest justification. And
I brought that hard club down.

The Family in the Hammock

The dog was under the hammock
the father was resting in
when the mother joined him
and started to swing.

And when the daughter joined them
and gave the hammock a spin
the dog sighed sweetly
under the hammock.

And when the son joined them
and the whole family grinned
the good dog sang
under the hammock.

And they swung and they swung
until the strings broke
and they laughed in the heap
of the hammock, not

realizing, at first,
as families sometimes don't,
the mischief they had wrung
on the forgotten dog

under the hammock.

As Time Goes By

after Onitsura

I do not know how to kiss, or I would kiss you. Where do noses go?

—INGRID BERGMAN

A kiss is a lovely trick, designed by nature to
stop speech when words become superfluous. Finally,
we're speechless. What else did Ingrid Bergman know?
Plenty, as it turns out. Like: *Be yourself. The*
world worships the original. Of course, her plum
role in the movie *Casablanca* is the one we all use
to identify her, although she referred to it only as "the
film I made with Bogart," insisting that on the whole
it was fine, but other films were dearer to her heart—
Spellbound, Notorious. In real life, she said, *I feel too*
big and clumsy. I can do everything with ease on stage. And
I don't think anyone has a right to intrude in your
life, but they do. And then Death made her his own.
He kissed her. He knew where to put his nose.

Turnips

after Issa

Our neighbor in the country has dementia. The
news roots in us, a sad and bitter turnip.
When first we bought our place he was the farmer
we sparred with, who, like a multiflora rose,
would, we thought, have taken all our land and
made it his own. When he showed up with
his guileless smile and artless speech, suggesting "a
guy" could do this or "a guy" could do that, fresh
from the city what could we do? His tractor pulled
onto our front lawn, the gift of a turnip
or some such in his hand, when he pointed
to something "a guy" could do, we took care to
keep him at bay. And now he leaves us alone. My
God! I listen for him coming down the road.

The Man in the Rain

after Buson

Sometimes things just slip out of existence: the
set of keys, the wallet, the cherished photo, all ferry
themselves off to who knows where? A thing departs
of its own accord, leaving you as bereft as
if it had intentionally abandoned you, the
vanishing enough to bring you down. The last
thing you want to be is to be left behind, the tardy
man whose friends and family have departed, the man
alone on the dock of his life, the man who stands
at a loss, unable quite to figure out what in
God's name has become of them. Which is the
most lost? That which is gone? Or that which first
noticed it missing? Summer, which sails off? Or winter,
which remains? The dear departed? Or the man in the rain?

The Red Fisherman

Why talk when you can paint?
    —Milton Avery

When the fisherman on the pier at Venice Beach,
casting for sheepshead and mullet, or maybe
mackerel or sea bass or bream,
catches a heron in the wing, and,
heartsick, chagrined, has no choice
but to play it slowly in, and
everyone in Sharkey's Bar puts down
their beer and conversation and looks on
as the stricken bird works
its way out to sea, and then,
exhausted, is pulled back in,
the scene around it turned severe,
everything stark and shadowless,
stopped in the freeze-framed sun,

what can we say about our mistakes,
our hungers, on this beautiful day,
how we're always getting caught
up in something we long to
extricate ourselves from—the harsh
word, the errant glare, the
unintended imprecation—how
sometimes a sentence unspools itself
like a length of monofilament line
cast into the faceless dark
equipped with its barbs and hooks,
to snag the world around us,
as if it didn't finally matter
what kind of chance we took?
There are sharks out there,
and herons.

Eventually, the fisherman
gives up and cuts the line, and,
like all things that finally escape us,
the heron lifts its wings and diminishes,
trailing the silvery thread of its reticence
as far as the eye can see, and we
go back to happy hour. Or do we
find ourselves standing on shore,
wondering what in God's name
we were angling for?

Real Men

I'm sitting on a bench on the boardwalk
at *Sharkey's on the Pier*, fishing gear
beside me—not mine, but that of two men
leaning over the rail, naked to the waist,
talking through the cigarettes clenched
between their broken teeth, greasy
dungarees and tattoos marking them
as men to be reckoned with.
Their expletives and laughter own the pier.
Now one has something on the line, something
big. Biceps straining, he plays it hard
across the Gulf, the water in the February
sun as bright as diamonds. And now an
eruption of froth—a shark breaking the surface
and then hauled in onto the deck between them
where it thrashes, primitive and fierce.
Now the other, all muscle and long bronzed
hair, forearm bandaged against a gash
he suffered and laughed off earlier,
grabs the shark barehanded, wrassles it
into submission, and, with his meaty fist,
punches it square in the snout. The shark is
down for the count, and the day stops
and holds its breath, as I sit, limp in my boots,
pale in the strident sun, out of my element,
pacifist that I am, thinking this is how
the world works, as somewhere off in
Iraq or Afghanistan, two men in a Humvee,
MK-47s at the ready, are taking on
an improvised roadside bomb. And then,
as if ending the afternoon show,
the man lets the stunned shark go.

Concealed Carry

after Basho

Two thugs with handguns walk into McDonald's. This
is not a joke. It's as if the dark
has walked in with them. The summer day turns autumn,
then dead of winter. The restaurant's crowded. An old
couple nervously makes room. What an age
we live in, where intimidation's handgun settles
everything. The swaggering men sit down
at what was the old folks' table. Their guns sit on
their hips like delinquent children. They stare at me
as I stare back at them. It's something like
a bad movie: the displaced couple, me, the heavy
thugs with guns. What was a sunny day clouds
over. Would words from me be punishment or
punch line? What are we to them but squirrels or birds?

Climate Change

after Basho

Late February, and yet the black-capped chickadees in
the morning are singing of spring; the finches at my
feeder are foraging; daffodils are lighting up the dark;
Bloodroot and Scylla are coming on strong. It's as if winter
were over, long gone. Is it global warming at last lying
in wait for us, the wind with a fever—and that ill
wind blowing no good? And yet, how lovely to look at
the trees leafing out, the cold season breathing its last,
the grass greening up like money! I think that I
could get used to this, sit back and not ask
any questions, though questions fester and bloom: How
long can we last without cold to contain us? How fares
the insect, the bacterium, the virus? Is it my
problem if the planet turns up the heat on my neighbor?

Never Again

How many times in the history of regret
have we heard that phrase: *never again!*
Given the mishap, the scandal, the disaster,
the unthinkable coming to pass
(*and how could it have happened?*)
we shake our collective heads.
We grow solemn. We're outraged, we're
incredulous. We trot our poor
sympathies out. And then

we set up our panels and commissions,
commence our investigations, issue
statements and advisories and reports.
We note that mistakes were made.
We remove the bad apples from the bin.
We put into place procedures,
institute new rules and regulations,
provide watchdogs and fail-safes,
backups and redundant systems.

We've all learned a painful lesson. Next time
we'll leave nothing to chance.
We'll get to the bottom of it. It
will never happen again.
And again. And again.

And Yet

after Basho and Issa

Basho was weighed down by the world. Shaking
with old age, autumn was his season. The
harvest moon, the heavy cloud, snow, the grave
mound were his favorite habitations. He was my
reliable confidante, my guide. Our one voice
tattered, abandoned, ruined, sad. Two autumn
frogs, plop! The sound of water, or of wind.
When Issa came along, singing, we were in
our usual funk, wondering what he would spring
on us next. An old woman, a caged bird, a cold rain
were, in his toothless mouth, as giddy as crickets. A
cow he was, mooing, mooing! An old man is a pretty
piece of work when he sees himself as a girl
or a peony! As for you, Death? There's Issa yawning.

III.

For Dear Life

Mumbo Jumbo

We were standing on the street corner,
our houses hard behind us in the snow,
and if we hadn't much to say, we could
always retreat to the safety of home.
It was a bit awkward; we were new
neighbors, so I told him about my poetry
(what little there was to know)
and he told me about his laboratory
research—how we would have the cure
for cancer, he said, in under twenty years.
He was pursuing every lead—radiation,
chemo, a voodoo woman in Haiti and
her curious potent herbs. I thought he
might be putting me on, but no, he said,
if mumbo jumbo works, then mumbo
jumbo. That was twenty years ago. And now
his wife is dead of a cancer diagnosed
just weeks ago. And what are we to do?
We're standing on the street corner,
shoveling snow, our houses hard behind us,
no one home. And he's still talking
science. And I'm still talking poetry.
Whatever mumbo jumbo gets us through.

After Basho

after Basho

There are over 100 translations of Basho's frog. The
literal version, phonetically, reads thus: *Fu-ru* (old)
i-ke (pond) *ya ka-wa-zu* (frog)—or, old pond
frog—*to-bi-ko-mu* (jumping into) *mi-zu* (water)—or, a
jumping into water—*no o-to* (sound). The frog
doesn't care if he's lost in translation. He jumps
anyway, and his meaning jumps with him. In
English, that frog water sound might be *kerplunk!*
I have my own small pond in the country. Now
and then, as I walk around it, a frog jumps in. The
sound it now makes, after Basho, is always the sound
of Basho's frog. The sound of the water is the sound of
his famous haiku, or "play verse," to translate the
term literally. An old pond. Basho jumps into the water.

After All

Every morning on my solitary walk to work
I see the great horned owl perched on its branch
outside the snow-covered hole in the old bur oak.
It's always there, no matter the time or the weather,
as I pass by bundled in parka and scarf and the woeful
wind chill of forty below. It sits, unmoved and unmoving,
gold eyes frozen in place, only its wind-twitched
ear tufts and eye feathers flickering. And I wonder
is it dreaming about whatever it is owls dream about—
rodents, small mammals, rabbits, and mice? Or
is that just more of *my* dreaming? For all I know
it could be stuffed, just a prank some wag under-
graduate placed on this branch behind his new dorm
to fool passersby like me. No matter. It's still, if you
will, a gift to see this owl on its perch, gazing at
whatever it is owls gaze at, thinking whatever it is
owls think, no matter which way the wind blows,
as if some things on this earth are here for keeps,
as if some things, at least, can be counted on
to live on in the eye of the beholder, even when
I, the beholder, have walked on deep into winter,
and walked on deeper, and am gone.

Happiness

is no warm puppy.
He's a sly dog, at best,
a mongrel, a cur, a beast
you can't count on
to do any of the tricks
you taught him to
through all the hard years.
Oh, he will fetch
when and what he wants to,
will even shake hands
and beg on occasion,
though, more often, he'll do
what he does best: circle,
roll over, play dead.

Which isn't to say
he won't occasionally
surprise you, follow you
home, faithfully lie
outside your door, snoring,
dreaming his doggy dreams
until you break down
and take him in, adopt him,
and, as if he were your
best friend, share your bed
and board, and stay up
all night together baying
at sadness, barking down
that cold, catty moon.

Goodness

said Mae West,
has nothing to do with it.
She was wrong.
In America, it's packaged
with freshness;
there's goodness
for goodness's sake.
If I buy it, it is
my goodness!
Sometimes it's gracious.
Honest! And
in some states it's just
a short drive from
Honest to Goodness.
I've done things
out of the goodness
of my heart.
Goodness me!
Goodness.
It's as American
as Mae West!
Goodness gracious
sakes alive!

Blowout Preventer

Ernie, age three, asks me
to help him "unwrap" his banana,
and, *sure*, I say, laughing, and as he
lifts up the half-peeled projectile
in all its improbable splendor, and
I grab it, the top breaks, and
Oh, no! You broke it! he wails, and
no joke, he's now inconsolable,
the banana collapsed in his hands,
his voice a loud smear in the air.
You broke it, he sobs, *now it's ruined!*
And I'm thinking of the Gulf oil spill,
how the platform exploded, all the fail-
safes failed, oil gushing up for months
into the Gulf's loop current
toward the Keys, everything dead
in its wake, and how this broken
banana, its thick skin discarded,
has blown up this small boy's trust
in a world of such breakage
where even a grandfather can fail,
and what can I do but put the peel
on my head and wear it, a last resort,
a "top hat" of sorts, and then pretend
to eat it, a "junk shot," a blowout preventer,
and by God, it works! as his wailing
disperses; he stops short,
his face a deep well of doubt
as his silence soaks up the moment.
And then our laughter seals the disaster
as we both spit the bad taste out.

This, Too, Shall Pass

Elsie, age three, sitting on my lap
on the porch at our country place,
says she'd like to have a beard like me
when she grows up someday.
Well, I say. *I don't think that you can.*
And *Why?* says she. And I
say *only boys have beards.* And she:
Okay, I'll be a boy! I'll be you
when I grow up, Grandpa Rusty!

I hadn't really wanted to be
here today. Had important work
to do, had been, anyway, a bit
down in the dumps of late
(a place that, at three,
I'd never have thought to be),
wondering what it's all about.
But now here I am, flying high,
with this small answer squirming
on my lap, happy to be alive!

Or, I'll be a worm! says she.
And slither through the grass!
And now we're lost in laughter
knowing this, too, soon shall pass.

Spiderwort

for Elsie, age five

When Elsie wants to know the name of that
plant out in the prairie with purple flowers,
"Spiderwort," I say, and "Oh," says she,
and then she wants to know why it's called that,
and when I say I don't know but maybe
it looks something like a spider, she
says, "Or it gives spiders warts?" Hours
later, back with a fistful of flowers, she

says she thinks she knows why it's called Spiderwort,
and "Why?" I say, and she stretches a thread
of milky sap in front of her as wide as her short
arms can reach, and there strings a web
of happiness as pure as any you'll ever see.
And I'm caught. Exactly where I want to be.

Durian Fruit

after Basho

It tastes like turpentine and old gym socks! they say. It
tastes more like fungi, I think, puréed parsnips, though skunk is
not so far off. A custardy duff, it's not unlike oysters.
It looks like a naked mole rat! they complain. I'm not
in complete disagreement: "You can eat them dried,"
I try, "but it's better to savor the glutinous smoothness." *Seaweed
paste!* they say. It's true. Not to mention the fecal smell that
gets them outlawed in public places. And yet: "Eat one
bite!" I say. "You'll want another. The 'King of Fruits' should
be distinctive!" Still, no matter how hard I try to sell
my granddaughters on my whimsies or pet nostalgias, when
one can choose jackfruit or the rose apple of youth, one
is hard put to want leaf mold, no matter how sweet it is.
They'll turn up their nose at the rank musty smell of the old.

Like, a Peony

after Issa

I tell her the *simile* begins with "like" or "as." The
way she said that pink flower was, *like, a peony,*
means it was *not* a peony. If it *was* a peony, it was,
well, a peony! I say. When she misuses "like" it's as
if she were speaking in similes. *It's, like, no big*
deal? she says. *Like, who really cares? Like, as*
long as you, like, know, like, what I'm saying? This
is, like, you know, like, a punctuation mark?, she says.
Like, it's, you know, just, like, a pause? Give us the
freedom to speak, like, you know, our own language? A little
toleration can go, like, you know, a long way? A girl,
can utilize, whatever she can, to get, like, an opening?
Like, what harm's in that? I think *she's* like a peony, her
face all pink and insistent-like. A peony up in arms.

O Shit!

after Basho

Sometimes we all feel shitty. Know we're all wet.
Look like shit. *Are* a shit. Have eaten a shit sandwich with
relish. I shit you not, it's worse than getting the
shits. So we just shit around, no shit, all morning,
and don't do shit, don't give a shit about anything. Dew
on the grass? Don't give us that shit. But shit happens, and
tough shit! When the shit hits the fan and you're splotched
with it? Sheee-it! Just get your shit together. Don't shit with
me, you piece of shit. You don't know shit from mud
(or Shinola, but who knows Shinola?). Holy Shit! *The
shit*, that's what we are! Life could be our melon,
our oyster (our road oyster, perhaps). So if it looks
like we're in deep shit, let's just shoot the shit. Especially
if first we can get shit-faced. Eat shit and die? Cool!

One-Liners

after Basho

I intend to live forever. So far, so good. His
regret: nostalgia isn't what it used to be. I figure
a day without sunshine is like night. Wishing
to play stupid with me? Don't. I'm better at it. To
err is human; to moo, bovine. It's bad luck, see,
to be superstitious. Whose idea was it to put an "s" in
lisp? Does this rag smell like chloroform to you? A
constipated man doesn't give a crap. Elvis is dead
and I'm not feeling too good myself. A successful tree
surgeon can't faint at the sight of sap. Without the
nipple, a breast would be pointless. The length
of the average man's penis is twice the length of
his thumb. Every man in the audience is now checking his
thumb. Dogs have a master; cats have a staff.

The Treatment

after Issa

She says I'm obsessive compulsive. But I'm not. I
just like things to be neat, in order. When I am
done counting the words in my sentence, she says she's envious
of my capacity for self-knowledge. I retort that her sarcasm's, of
course, passive aggressive. *Will you listen to him?*
she says, mock incredulous. *My loving husband. The man who
can do no wrong. Who everyone loves. Who, by the way, is
also manic depressive.* I'M! NOT! I shout! NOT! BEING!
MANIC! I'm feeling sorry for myself for being scolded,
too down to point out her borderline personality, the
attention deficit disorder that could be the end
of us as she bounces from room to room. *But think of
your Asperger's!* she offers. YOUR AUTISM! I thrust. And the
treatment keeps us going, year after year after year.

Swiss Chard

And when I see we don't have any lettuce
for my sandwich, I ask my wife, and she
says, *Why don't you just go out into the garden
and get some fresh Swiss chard?* And so I go
out into the garden and see what looks like
cabbage (though it's October and by now
it could be anything), and what looks like
broccoli (or the remains of it), and maybe shards
of rhubarb, maybe parsley, and one of these
must be Swiss chard, but I'm not sure,
and feeling ignorant: How can a man of sixty-six
not know what Swiss chard is? So I bring in
a small assortment of leaves, hoping one will do,
and she just laughs, derisively, and says,
You think that that's Swiss chard?
Come on, you know what Swiss chard is!
And, *Of course, I do,* I say, eating my weedy
sandwich. *It's a joke!* But I don't, any more
than I know a host of other things she thinks
I know that keep our garden growing,
that are all Swiss chard to me.

Sex at Seventy

after Issa

This morning they're having a rollicking good time in
bed, doing things they haven't done in years. My
goodness! You'd think they'd want to keep this hidden
from public view: what happens in the house
they'd keep in the house; they'd be discreet. But no,
here they are unveiling lips and tongue and teeth
until nothing that they could possibly do is left
to anyone's imagination. Come on in
and join us, they say. You there! Yes, you! Who says the
old aren't sexual beings, too? Is your mouth
filled with laughter? We're laughing, too, but
it's a beatific laughter, laughter so feel-good
it becomes us. We *are* laughter! And, with luck,
we *will be* laughter, no matter what abounds.

You, Love

after Basho

When everything seems too much for me and I'm walking
a thin line between sanity and madness—I'm on
the edge, the world is weighing me down and
I think I won't survive, I'm all but through, I'm on
my last legs, people around me are failing me, even
the people I love most keep knocking me down, try though
I may to pick myself up and try again, and I
know the worst is upon me, know what it is to fall
to my knees in supplication, praying to be let down
easy, and I know what it is to be defeated, sick
of it all, unto death, helpless, hopeless, and finally in
no shape to rise to any occasion—whole fields
of failure unfold before me until I manage to think of
you, my meadow, my stream, my field of sweet clover.

String Theory

I have to believe a Beethoven
string quartet is not unlike
the elliptical music of gossip:
one violin excited
to pass its small story along
to the next violin and the next
until, finally, come full circle,
the whole conversation is changed.

And I have to believe such music
is at work at the deep heart of things,
that under the protons and electrons,
behind the bosons and quarks,
with their bonds and strange attractors,
these strings, these tiny vibrations,
abuzz with their big ideas,
are filling the universe with gossip,
the unsung art of small talk

that, not unlike busybody Beethoven,
keeps us forever together, even
when everything's flying apart.

My Last Poem

And by that I do not mean
my previous poem, my poem
before this one, my recently completed
poem. I mean my *last* poem, as in
terminal, the end, all done, *fini*.
I do hope, of course, that
this last poem will last, as if crafted
on a "last," one of the last words you'd expect
to show up in a poem that does not want
to give anyone the boot, or shoe
anyone away, but wants to bring forth a
"load" or "cargo," a "last," say, of
codfish, white herring, or ash, a "last"
of gunpowder, wool, or tar (this last
poem should carry a lot).
And I do hope this ship will
not come in last, but will instead last
and last, and last (but not least), will make
a lasting impression, this poem that is,
have I said it? my last. And lest I be
the last to admit it: at last!
my last will and testament, my last laugh,
my famous last words.

Rounded With a Sleep

after Issa

My two-year-old granddaughter won't go to bed. Life,
she thinks, is too good to sleep away, so, suddenly, she is
loquacious. Things that had held no interest all day—a
wooden block, a plastic doll, a piece of lint, a dewdrop,
are now worthy of her full attention. Oh, yes,
she is much too busy to attend to her mother, and I
am but a small annoyance, an impediment. I am
of little consequence. Bedtime? She's not convinced.
And so we sit back and let her regale us. Life
is something she knows a lot about. She is
talking on and on to herself, she is a stream, a
flow, an ocean of talk, and we are but a dewdrop.
It's late. We know this is going to have to end, and
we're going to have to convince her. And yet, and yet.

Dear Life

This morning on my way out the door
to fetch the morning newspaper,
I found a lucky penny. When
I opened the paper up,
all the news was good!
So I went to the endodontist,
in hopes that she could fix
the bite a new dentist
had badly screwed up.
I hadn't eaten (comfortably) in weeks.
My mouth was full of marbles,
asymmetrical, askew. *What can
you do?* I asked her, and she
ground some high spots down
with her trusty dental burr.
How's that? she said. *I'm no
expert in occlusion.* But she was!
My bite was almost perfect! I
went home and suited up
in my track and garden suit. I
weeded my morning glories. I
went for my afternoon run. For
the first time all year I finished
the four miles without stopping.
I was wonderfully exhausted,
slick with sweat and exultation.
My wife was especially beautiful.
We went out to eat at Samba,
where cute Brazilian boys served
every kind of meat off
steel and wooden skewers. It was
the first pleasant meal I'd had
in weeks. So much for toothless
diets. So much for mashed potatoes,
Jell-O, pudding, cream of wheat.

Bring me pork loin, flank steak,
leg of lamb, roast beef. Here,
take my lucky penny. You look
like you could use it! You, too,
can grace the headlines, you can be
a headliner. All the news is good.
So's the roast beef.
I'm applauding with my teeth!

Notes

The sonnets spread throughout this book, designated by the presence of epigraphs such as "after Basho" and "after Issa" and so on, are built on haiku. The last words of each line of each poem, read vertically from top to bottom, form a haiku by a classical Japanese master.

The haiku that inform these poems are drawn from the following sources (please note that I've also included in parentheses which poems each source informs). My thanks to the translators for permission to reprint their translations:

Beilenson, Peter. *Japanese Haiku.* White Plains, NY: Peter Pauper Press, 2012. ("Turnips" and "Good Lord"). Reprinted from *Japanese Haiku*, trans. Peter Beilenson, first published in 1955 and republished as an ebook in 2012 by Peter Pauper Preess, Inc. www.peterpauper.com. Used by permission.

Hamill, Sam. *The Sound of Water: Haiku by Basho, Buson, Issa, and Other Poets.* Boston: Shambhala, 1995. ("Wolf Pack," "As Time Goes By," "The Man in the Rain," "Concealed Carry," "O Shit!," and "Sex at Seventy"). Socho ["The moon this evening,"], Onitsura ["To finally know"], Buson ["The ferry departs"], Basho ["This dark autumn"] and ["Wet with morning dew"], and Issa ["In my hidden house"], from *The Sound of Water: Haiku by Basho, Buson, Issa and Other Poets*, translated by Sam Hamill, 1995 by Sam Hamill. Reprinted by arrangement with The Permissions Company, Inc., on behalf of Shambhala Publications, Inc., Boston, MA. www.shambhala.com

Hass, Robert. *The Essential Haiku: Versions of Basho, Buson, and Issa.* New Jersey: Ecco Press, 1994. ("The Andromeda Galaxy" and "And Yet"). Haiku on pp. 14 (Basho), 171 (Issa), from *The Essential Haiku: Versions of Basho, Busson & Issa,* edited and with an introduction by Robert Hass. Introduction and selection copyright © 1994 by Robert Hass. Unless otherwise noted, all translations copyright © 1994 by Robert Hass. Reprinted by permission of HarperCollins Publishers.

Reichold, Jane. *Basho: The Complete Haiku.* New York: Kodansha International, 2008. ("Shine God's Light," "Sweet Potatoes," "Durian Fruit," and "One-Liners"). Reprinted by permission of Kodansha USA, Inc. Excerpted from *Basho: The Complete Haiku* by Jane Reichhold, copyright © 2008, 2013 by Jane Reichhold.

thegreenleaf.co.uk/Japanese_Masters.htm. ("The Rapture," "Song of Myself," "You Bet Your Life," "Climate Change," "And Yet," "Like, a Peony," "The Treatment," "You, Love," and "Rounded with a Sleep")

Acknowledgments

The author would like gratefully to acknowledge the editors of the following publications in which some of these poems originally appeared (sometimes in slightly different form):

Birmingham Poetry Review: "God's Grace"; *Blackbird*: "The Rapture"; *Black Warrior Review*: "Hunger"; *Blue Unicorn*: "My Last Poem"; *Carolina Quarterly*: "Dear Life" (originally "Occlusion"); *Crab Orchard Review*: "Catching My Father"; *Hampden-Sydney Review*: "The Andromeda Galaxy," "You Bet Your Life"; *Hubbub*: "Wolf Pack"; *In Posse Review*: "Blowout Preventer," "Swiss Chard"; *Lindenwood Review*: "Mumbo Jumbo"; *Margie*: "The Day My Father Said 'Shit'"; *Nimrod International Journal*: "After Basho," "Durian Fruit," "The Man in the Rain," "Sex at Seventy"; *Ontario Review*: "Never Again"; *Poem*: "And Yet" (originally "Furthermore"), "The Biography of Nostalgia," "Rounded with a Sleep," "Spiderwort"; *Poet Lore*: "Bed Wetter," "The Knowing," "Turnips"; *Poetry East*: "Geologic"; *Poetry Northwest*: "Real Men," "In the Great Scheme of Things"; *Ploughshares*: "Song of Myself"; *Redactions*: "String Theory"; *Southern Review*: "The Red Fisherman" (originally "Heron"); *Sou'wester*: "Concealed Carry," "Modes of Transport"; *Spillway*: "The Treatment"; *Spirituality and Health*: "This, Too, Shall Pass"; *Sycamore Review*: "Scrabble"; *Texas Review*: "Like, a Peony"; *Verse Wisconsin*: "Body World," "Climate Change"

Thanks to the Graduate School of the University of Wisconsin-Madison for grants that assisted the completion of this book.

Special thanks to Ed Ochester for over thirty years of friendship and good advice.